C000268693

FRANCIS FRITH'S

TOWN & CITY

MEMORIES

ILKLEY

ROBERT PREEDY'S schooldays were spent in Chesterfield, also Francis Frith's home town. He has spent his working life in broadcasting with both the BBC and ITV. His various jobs have included cameraman, researcher and promotions producer. He was also a continuity announcer for thirteen years at Yorkshire Television in Leeds. Currently he presents a weekly music show for regional BBC. With his keen interest in local studies, he has published numerous books and articles on Yorkshire history from Victorian times. Away from broadcasting and writing, his business interests have included running two cinemas. The first was in Pickering from 1984, and the second in Wetherby where he now lives.

FRANCIS FRITH'S
TOWN & CITY
MEMORIES

ILKLEY

ROBERT PREEDY

FRANCIS FRITH'S

TOWN & CITY

MEMORIES

First published as Ilkley, A Photographic History of your Town
in 2001 by Black Horse Books, an imprint of The Francis Frith Collection
Revised edition published in the United Kingdom in 2006 by
The Francis Frith Collection as Ilkley, Town and City Memories
Limited Hardback Edition ISBN 1-84589-126-0
Paperback Edition ISBN 1-84589-127-9

Text and Design copyright ° The Francis Frith Collection®
Photographs copyright ° The Francis Frith Collection®
except where indicated

The Frith® photographs and the Frith® logo are reproduced under licence from
Heritage Photographic Resources Ltd, the owners of the Frith® archive and trademarks.
'The Francis Frith Collection', 'Francis Frith' and 'Frith' are registered trademarks of Heritage
Photographic Resources Ltd.

All rights reserved. No photograph in this publication may be sold to a third party other
than in the original form of this publication, or framed for sale to a third party.
No parts of this publication may be reproduced, stored in a retrieval system, or transmitted,
in any form, or by any means, electronic, mechanical, photocopying, recording or otherwise,
without the prior permission of the publishers and copyright holder

British Library Cataloguing in Publication Data

Ilkley
Town and City Memories
Robert Preedy

The Francis Frith Collection®
Frith's Barn, Teffont,
Salisbury, Wiltshire SP3 5QP
Tel: +44 (0) 1722 716 376
Email: info@francisfrith.co.uk
www.francisfrith.co.uk

Aerial photographs reproduced under licence from Simmons Aerofilms Limited
Historical Ordnance Survey maps reproduced under licence from Homecheck.co.uk

Printed and bound in England

Front Cover: **ILKLEY, THE GROVE c1965** I6096t
The colour-tinting in this image is for illustrative purposes only,
and is not intended to be historically accurate

Every attempt has been made to contact copyright holders of illustrative material.
We will be happy to give full acknowledgement in future editions for any items not credited.
Any information should be directed to The Francis Frith Collection.

AS WITH ANY HISTORICAL DATABASE, THE FRANCIS FRITH ARCHIVE IS CONSTANTLY
BEING CORRECTED AND IMPROVED, AND THE PUBLISHERS WOULD WELCOME
INFORMATION ON OMISSIONS OR INACCURACIES

FRANCIS FRITH'S
TOWN & CITY
MEMORIES

CONTENTS

Francis Frith, Victorian founder of the world-famous photographic archive, was a devout Quaker and a highly successful Victorian businessman. By 1860 he was already a multi-millionaire, having established and sold a wholesale grocery business in Liverpool. He had also made a series of pioneering photographic journeys to the Nile region. The images he returned with were the talk of London. An eminent modern historian has likened their impact on the population of the time to that on our own generation of the first photographs taken on the surface of the moon.

Frith had a passion for landscape, and was as equally inspired by the countryside of Britain as he was by the desert regions of the Nile. He resolved to set out on a new career and to use his skills with a camera. He established a business in Reigate as a specialist publisher of topographical photographs.

Frith lived in an era of immense and sometimes violent change. For the poor in the early part of Victoria's reign work was a drudge and the hours long, and ordinary people had precious little free time. Most had not travelled far beyond the boundaries of their own town or village. Mass tourism was in its infancy during the 1860s, but during the next decade the railway network and the establishment of Bank Holidays and half-Saturdays gradually made it possible for the working man and his family to enjoy holidays and to see a little more of the world. With characteristic business acumen, Francis Frith foresaw that these new tourists would enjoy having souvenirs to commemorate their days out. He began selling photo-souvenirs of seaside resorts and beauty spots, which the Victorian public pasted into treasured family albums.

Frith's aim was to photograph every town and village in Britain. For the next thirty years he travelled the country by train and by pony and trap, producing fine photographs of seaside resorts and beauty spots that were keenly bought by millions of Victorians.

THE RISE OF FRITH & CO

Each photograph was taken with tourism in mind, the small team of Frith photographers concentrating on busy shopping streets, beaches, seafronts, picturesque lanes and villages. They also photographed buildings: the Victorian and Edwardian eras were times of huge building activity, and town halls, libraries, post offices, schools and technical colleges were springing up all over the country. They were invariably celebrated by a proud Victorian public, and photo souvenirs – visual records – published by F Frith & Co were sold in their hundreds of thousands. In addition, many new commercial buildings such as hotels, inns and pubs were photographed, often because their owners specifically commissioned Frith postcards or prints of them for re-sale or for publicity purposes.

In order to gain some understanding of the scale of Frith's business one only has to look at the catalogue issued by Frith & Co in 1886: it runs to some 670 pages. By 1890 Frith had created the greatest specialist photographic publishing company in the world, with over 2,000 stockists! The picture on the right shows the Frith & Co display board on the wall of the stockist at Ingleton in the Yorkshire Dales (left of window). Beautifully constructed with a mahogany frame and gilt inserts, it displayed a dozen scenes.

POSTCARD BONANZA

The ever-popular holiday postcard we know today took many years to appear, and F Frith & Co was in the vanguard of its development. Postcards became a hugely popular means of communication and sold in their millions. Frith's company took full advantage of this boom and soon became the major publisher of photographic view postcards.

Francis Frith died in 1898 at his villa in Cannes, his great project still growing. His sons Eustace and Cyril continued their father's monumental task, expanding the number of views offered to the public and recording more and more places in Britain, as the coasts and countryside were opened up to mass travel. The archive Frith created continued in business for another seventy years. By 1970 it contained over a third of a million pictures of 7,000 cities, towns and villages. The massive photographic record Frith has left to us stands as a living monument to a special and very remarkable man.

This book shows Ilkley as it was photographed by this world-famous archive at various periods in its development over the past 150 years. Every photograph was taken for a specific commercial purpose, which explains why the selection may not show every aspect of the town landscape. However, the photographs, compiled from one of the world's most celebrated archives, provide an important and absorbing record of your town.

ILKLEY FROM THE AIR 1928 AF24362

INTRODUCING ILKLEY

WELCOME to the charming town of Ilkley - a town that rather likes to hide its historical gems. With this book of atmospheric photographs, you'll discover the people and buildings that put the town firmly on the Victorian resort map. Ilkley's fame is based on one ordinary item - water. Water for the spa and water for the steam railway. Of course the location beneath the moors and nestling in the river valley helped, yet even the Romans knew Ilkley without being aware of its spa potential. Without the wealth of the industrial West Ridings, it's possible that the town might have remained a small and insignificant village. With the waters discovered, it was the town's pre-eminence in the world of the hydro that attracted the wealthy during the mid-1800s. During this period medical knowledge was rapidly increasing and becoming a major discussion topic in journals and newspapers. While the health of the workers was a concern for many reformers, it was the informed and wealthy who were first to spend their Yorkshire brass on medical cures.

The novel idea of using something as natural as water to cleanse and purify the body arrived here via Austria. Malvern was the first English town to thrive on its natural spa water, but soon afterwards many other spas were established: Matlock, Bath, Cheltenham and Harrogate, to name but a few.

Seeing the possibility of a spa in the Wharfe Valley, a former Mayor of Leeds, Hamer Stansfeld, and three other Leeds businessmen chose a 65-acre site in nearby Wheatley for their magnificent Ben Rhydding Hydro. Guests arrived here on horse-drawn coaches from Leeds and Bradford; within a few years the Hydro had its own special railway station.

THE TOWN 1900 45162A

A hundred years after this photograph was taken, there appears to have been little change to the overall shape of the town, for Ilkley today retains the charm of the Wharfe Valley and the splendour of Rombalds moor. This vista from Middleton clearly illustrates how the town has skilfully avoided any urban sprawl. From the Cow and Calf rocks, top left, down past the Ben Rhydding Hydro, and then along the Grove with the Spa Hydro, Ilkley must have been a breathtaking experience for turn of the century visitors, who were perhaps more used to the cramped and smoky surroundings of the industrial West Ridings.

BEN RHYDDING 1886 18562

We are now high above the famous Cow and Calf Rocks looking down the eastern side of Ilkley with the Ben Rhydding Hydro dominating the original hamlet of Wheatley, which was renamed once the hydro opened for business on 29 May 1844. Costing £30,000, this was the very first purpose built hydro in this country.

The success of Ben Rhydding led to a boom in the building of many more hydrotherapy centres in Ilkley. The acclaimed Leeds architect, Cuthbert Brodrick, was invited to design the stunning Wells House high up on the side of the moor. Less grand and less expensive establishments rapidly came into business, and by the late 1800s Ilkley had become the chosen centre for refined socialising. Pierrot shows and musical concerts gave the town the year-round air of a successful holiday resort.

When the railway arrived in the mid-1800s, the town became even more popular. Visitors streaming from the trains were greeted by the splendid complex comprising the Town Hall, Carnegie Library, Winter Gardens and King's Hall. Easy access from the West Ridings also encouraged the well-to-do to reside in the town; a second building boom then transformed the southern part of the town leading from the Grove up to the moor. Here solid new Yorkshire houses were snapped up by the wealthy who could now ignore the industrial desolation of the mill towns where they had made their money. Here in Ilkley, the views were uninterrupted and the air was smoke free.

And so it has remained to this day. Industry has been kept at bay, the council shows due respect to the town's heritage and the residents stay ever vigilant against unsuitable developments.

In this book, step back into a time devoid of traffic jams, where life was lived at a leisurely pace and the industrial north could be forgotten. Francis Frith's splendid photographs, taken over a period of a hundred years, capture Ilkley at its majestic best.

THE GROVE

THE GROVE really was the place to be seen, and a promenade was an essential part of the relaxed social life of the town. Here you could stop and pause at the splendid cafés: the Imperial, the Kiosk and the Spa. Handsome shops catered for the affluent visitor. Here you would find milliners, first-class grocers, a cabinetmaker, needlework and artist suppliers, a bookseller, a glass and china shop, a photographers and a piano showroom. All the major banks of the day were conveniently grouped at the start of the Grove, which marked the boundary between the residential and commercial areas of the town. Originally known as Green Lane, it retained a collection of farm buildings and cottages until as late as 1891. The charming Green Lane Cottage was demolished in that year to make way for more shops; the cottage site is now Betty's Cafe and Tearooms, in line with the tradition of genteel relaxation and refreshment.

Photograph 63556 shows us the very heart of the town as it was before the First World War, with shoppers in relaxed mood sampling the splendid shops of the Grove. This was the era of pedal and horsepower but the open top tourer was certainly a possession to aspire to. The financial businesses are on the left of the view - the London, City and Midland Bank is today occupied by an estate agency. Further down is the Craven Bank, which later became Martin's Bank and is now a building society. The Congregational Church still exists, but the Spa Hydro just behind was demolished in 1989. On the right A Duckworth, Pharmaceutical Chemist, is now a chocolate shop. Mason's butcher shop, previously Joseph Moon's, was later run by Percy Dalton, but is today split into an estate agent and a jewellers.

The Congregational Church, opened in June 1869 at a cost of £6,119, is here still several decades away from the

The Grove 1911 63556

interior reconstruction that took place in the mid-1980s for a staggering £250,000. Now it is known as the Christchurch Methodist and United Reformed Church.

View I6026, pages 18-19, shows the delightful fountain at the bottom of Mill Ghyll, once a very impressive affair until repeated vandalism forced the council to prune the top half in 1959. Today even the little lake has been replaced by easy maintenance flowerbeds. By the time of this photograph, the horse carriage is nowhere to be seen, but the car has started to gobble up The Grove's parking space.

Built as part of the Charity Hospital in 1862, the Convalescent Hospital (see 74474A, pages 22-23) served the town well, offering a mixture of convalescent rooms and hospital wards, with personal care from your own GP. During the First World War, the home was commandeered by the army as a military hospital. Many Belgian soldiers were first to recuperate here; later, the town saw the effect of the war on its own troops as many British personnel came here to forget the horror of the trenches.

There was much sadness in the town when financial cuts forced the hospital's closure in 1993. On the final day, Wednesday 31st March, Matron Sheila Wormald cleared her desk and commented, 'The place just echoes now - it's horrible'. Happily the Victorian Gothic-Revival building was reopened late 2004 as an integrated care facility by the national charity, Abbeyfield, after a £9 million refurbishment project.

Photograph I6087, pages 26-27, is taken further west along the Grove. The old Spa Hydro is on the right, built in 1864 as the Grove Hydropathic Establishment, and renamed the Spa in 1885. It catered for visitors who wished to avoid too much energetic walking - all the other hydros were further

THE GROVE 1921 71265

Ten years and one world war later, time seems to have stood still in the town. We can see the horse carriage gently manoeuvring out of Brook Street, only pausing for a few solitary cars. Hargreaves' cycle shop on the left appears to be bravely ignoring the impending domination of the Grove by the automobile.

from the centre of the charming Grove. The Spa was converted into flats in 1910 but was sadly demolished in 1989. New luxurious apartments appeared the following year.

Ilkley offers many convenient places to relax. The gardens shown next to the spa are at the bottom of Parish Ghyll Road.

At the west end of the Grove are a number of small but inviting parks. Parish Ghyll Park (see 79053, pages 28-29), which looks huge in this view, is today slightly less luxuriant and more open, although rather more compact than suggested here. The seats in the centre are now built up as a bed of flowers and shrubs.

At the end of the Grove, just beyond the Memorial Gardens, are Spence's Gardens, a delightful oasis given to the town by one Doctor Spence from the nearby village of Weston. As shown in the first view (56477, pages 24-25), nannies could walk here to sun their charges, small children could cause mischief and old men could scrutinise the daily newspaper headlines. In the background is the King's Road Baptist Church built in 1902.

In view 75097, page 28, almost two decades later, Spence's Gardens has lost none of its charm. Native and tropical plants give this summer view an air of old England. On the left we can glimpse Morven House. Further up Grove Road is Heathcote, possibly Ilkley's finest house. It was designed by Edwin Lutyens and built in 1906 at a cost of £17,500 for textile magnate Mr J Hemingway. By 1956 it had been sold for use as offices, and today we can be thankful that the exterior and grounds have not been altered in any way.

THE GROVE c1955 16026

THE GROVE C1965 16096

Shown here, just past the Congregational Church, is the lower part of the cultivated gardens of the Convalescent Hospital. Colourful flower beds provided relaxing views and the seats helped to rest weary legs after an energetic march up to the moors. An attractive bandstand has since been constructed on the lower part of the hospital gardens. On the north side of the Grove, the cars in this view are no longer all black, with the range of shapes and colours reflecting the fashionable designs of driving.

THE GROVE

THE CONVALESCENT HOSPITAL 1923 74474A

SPENCE'S GARDENS 1906 56477

THE GROVE

Above: THE GROVE c1965 16087

Right: SPENCE'S GARDENS
1925 79057

Far Right: CHALYBEATE SPRING
1921 71273

On the western fringe of the town, a very pleasant walk leads up the wooded valley to Panorama rocks. Just below the moors is this rustic old well in Heber's Ghyll. The land was given to the town in 1887 by the Lord of the Manor, Charles Marmaduke Middleton.

PARISH GHYLL PARK 1925 79053

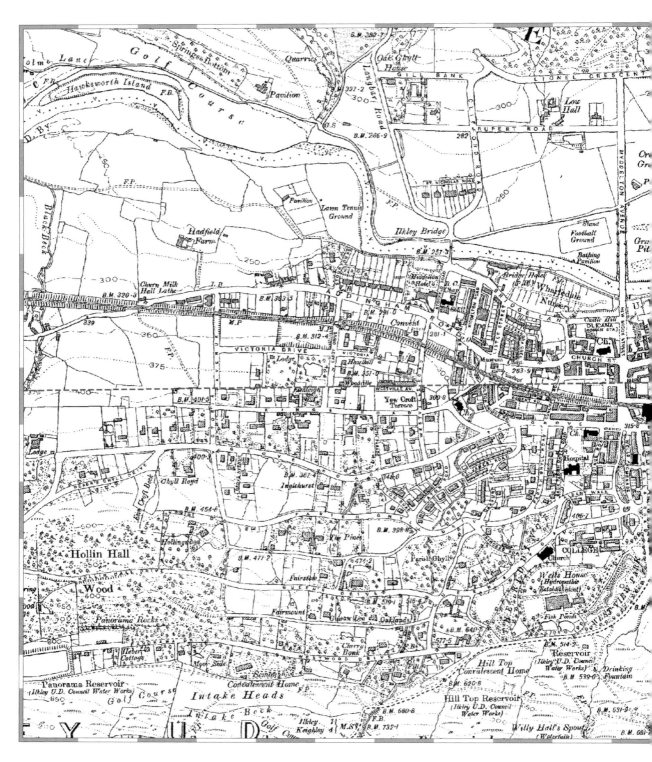

An Ordnance Survey Map Showing Ilkley And Surrounding Areas 1907

THE RAILWAY STEAMS IN

THE TWENTY-TWO mile railway between Arthington and Skipton took some time to arrive. As early as 1847, an attempt had been made, but with costs estimated at £420,000 this was soon abandoned. Railway-mania may have gripped the nation but by the time of the Ilkley schemes, the era of wild optimism to connect ever-smaller towns and villages was fast running out of steam.

Yet entrepreneurs still had their sights on a line to join the Leeds and Bradford lines to Lancashire, for the great industrial powerhouses demanded access to greater markets. A further scheme was devised: the North Eastern Railway would construct the line through Pool and Otley to Burley, while the Midland Railway would extend the line from Apperley Bridge through Guiseley to Burley, where the two would meet. From here, the joint company would take the line through to Ilkley on to Skipton,

BROOK STREET 1906 56473

Leeds and five to Bradford, while three extras made the seven-mile journey to Otley. After 1866, Ben Rhydding also had its own special station, requested and paid for by the Hydro.

Next, a further eleven miles of track to Skipton were planned at a cost of £302,000. The famous girder bridge took the line forward from Ilkley station towards a massive viaduct running along the back of the Grove through the gap now occupied by the Clarke Foley centre.

Bolton Abbey station was opened on 16th May 1888, just in time for the summer trade to this beauty spot. By October passengers could continue their journey through Embsay to Skipton. This final section is still open as a preserved railway and much effort has recently gone into a complete rebuilding of Bolton Abbey station.

The perfect public transport system was now in place for goods and passenger traffic between the West Ridings and the fresh air of the Dales. This was to become the major driving force for the residential development of Ilkley. Wealthy mill owners and merchants from the smoke-filled towns of industrial Yorkshire could now escape the pollution produced by their own factories. Ilkley's Victorian boom-time began: sturdy new houses were built just off the Grove and much of today's town was established within just a few years of the railway's arrival.

A century later and the rise of car ownership started to affect trade on the trains. The Beeching axe was wielded, with branch lines being hit the hardest: passenger links from Ilkley to Skipton and from Ilkley to Arthington were severed on 22nd March 1965. Brook Street reverted to its 19th century appearance when the latticed railway bridge was removed in 1966. The service from Ilkley to Leeds and Bradford remains today, but it has been won only through a long and determined fight by the town's residents.

where it would meet the Bradford, Shipley, Saltaire and Keighley line.

Poor weather led to many delays but Otley was finally reached and the first train steamed into the town on 1st February 1865. Ilkley station opened just a few months later on 1st August - the town was hung with bunting and much celebration took place. A staff of 24 ran the busy Ilkley terminus and each day six trains went to

BROOK STREET

BEFORE 1853 Brook Street didn't exist, this area being merely the riverbed of the Mill Ghyll stream that flowed off the moor on a direct route to the Wharfe. In 1853, the stream was diverted below ground and its former course redeveloped into modern Brook Street. Houses on either side were quickly converted to commercial premises and by the early 1860s the shape of today's street was formed - although thatched cottages and farm buildings remained until the turn of the century. Brook Street was always more commercial and down to earth than the Grove: here you would find a fishmonger, grocer, butcher, cobbler, a fancy goods store, a chemist and a draper.

Gothic House, built near the bottom of the street on the site of an old farm in 1870, was first used by John Shuttleworth as a stationers. Later he published the Ilkley Gazette newspaper from here. Gothic House in its latter years was the Fish Dish and is now Boots the Chemist. At the junction of Brook Street with Leeds Road and Church Street were three public houses - the Star and the adjoining Wharfedale, and then, next to the church, the Wheatsheaf - all offering plenty of choice to eager drinkers.

Originally Brook Street had a brook running through it. This stream from Mill Ghyll was diverted into a culvert in 1853, leaving a wide bed upon which a commercial street was formed. Fifty years before photograph 56473 (pages 30-31) was taken, Brook Street was little more than a dusty track, turning to a muddy quagmire during the autumn and winter months.

Mason's butcher's shop on the corner with the Grove still dominates the scene, but the railway bridge gives this view of Brook Street a distinctive Victorian feel. The full variety of transport still co-existed and by this time, the railway was bringing visitors to the town; the horse carriages would wait to take them up to the moors and the

many hydros and guest houses. The open top car illustrates the growing wealth of residents who could now commute daily to their factories in Leeds and Bradford. Ilkley life just after the Boer War was a time of genteel living, straw boaters and Hovis bread.

The gas light on the right was introduced under the Town Lighting Act of 1866 and was first lit in August the following year.

Further down Brook Street, towards the river, was the more day-to-day shopping area. Here you could browse

32

Above: Brook Street 1911 63557

In this photograph, taken a few years after 56473 (pages 30-31), horse carriages still await their fares in the centre of Brook Street. Just opposite are the offices of the Wharfedale Moor Cab Company, now demolished. Nearby is the site of the forthcoming 1930s Woolworth store and 1980s redevelopment. Down past the latticed railway bridge is the new road over the bridge to Middleton. At this time, before the First World War, the town is still very relaxed.

Left: Extract from Brook Street 1906 56473

BROOK STREET

the freshly caught game at Hampshire's Fruit and Game Salesroom (see 16079, pages 36-37). Next door on the left in photograph 63558, pages 34-35, is the Wharfedale Café, then the opticians, the silversmith and the watchmakers. On the right is Hudson's the boot and shoemaker. At the end of Brook Street on the left is the Wheatsheaf Hotel, one of many that used to be clustered around this important throughway from Leeds to Skipton. The Wheatsheaf was finally demolished in 1959 to allow gardens to be added to the churchyard. The Star can be seen on the opposite corner of Leeds Road.

The main road along the Wharfe from Otley comes into the town at this point. Two major hotels greeted travellers: the Crescent (56474, pages 38-39, out of shot on the right) offered drivers a Motor Garage complete with inspection pit; and the Star of Wharfedale, shown here a year after its opening in 1905. Two old public houses, the old Star and the Wharfedale at the rear of the new Star were later demolished, opening up New Brook Street for development.

BROOK STREET 1911 63558

BROOK STREET C1965 16079

Ford, Morris, Hillman and Triumph - all the big automobile names are represented here as the town becomes accustomed to the motor age. Banking premises have started to squeeze out independent retailers, while the Woolworth store heralds the era of bargain shopping. However, the town still considers the comforts of the individual visitor through the provision of seats and flowerbeds. By the time this photo was taken the railway had closed. The Beeching plan axed the Otley to Skipton line via Ilkley with the final through train on Saturday 20th March 1965. Buffer stops were added to the Ilkley station on 3rd January 1966 and the eighty year old bridge over Brook Street was demolished, with work starting at 5am on Sunday 10th July 1966.

THE STAR HOTEL AND LEEDS ROAD
1906 56474

EARLY MAN AND THE ROMANS

FLINTS found on the moor are evidence of early man. Since the mid-Stone age, people have settled in this area of the valley. Neolithic man came here and by the Bronze age (1500-400 BC) their sophistication led to artistic patterns being carved on the rocks - the swastika stone and the cup and ring carvings make Ilkley unique in this country. The marks on the stones suggest religious and fertility rites.

Each new archaeological dig offers yet more clues to the early history of the valley. During the Iron Age, the foundations of modern Ilkley were laid. Village life revolved around a field system of agriculture with farmers using axes and ploughs. Clothing was produced using spinning and weaving. By this time horses were harnessed for their immense power - a sight not unfamiliar around the fields of fifty years ago. Building material for domestic and farming use was quarried from around the Cow and Calf rocks. During the Iron Age, the name of Llecan was edging nearer to the Roman town name of Olicana.

In AD43 Roman troops landed in Kent and began their gradual containment of our country. Their first road north was to Colchester - they then took their skills further up country to Lincoln, Brough and York. Under Governor Agricola a fort was established midway between York and Manchester at the head of the Wharfe valley. Olicana was the chosen name for the settlement and this was the first formal settlement of the town we know as Ilkley. A wooden fort was established in a sheltered part of the valley, near to the Wharfe but with a commanding view to all sides. On this two-acre site, the Romans marked out their territory for their eventual aim of quelling any rebellion by the Brigantes - tough northern warriors. Auxiliary workers were housed just

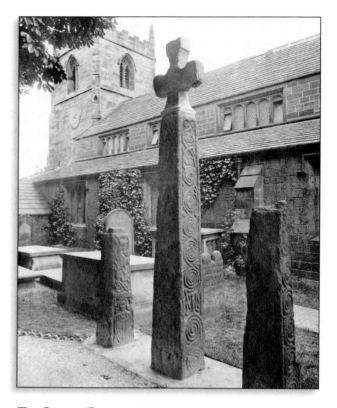

THE SAXON CROSSES 1916 67326

south of the fort in the area around the present day Grove Convalescent Home. During the building of the colossal Hadrian's Wall, many troops from Ilkley were sent marching northwards.

Ilkley's fort was effectively abandoned in the years AD122-125. Never again did it hold much importance, its stature being much reduced when it was rebuilt as a signal station. By AD410, all remaining troops were withdrawn as the Romans trudged back to deal with unrest in their homelands. Many artefacts have been since found within the site of the fort. Archaeological surveys were held in 1919-1922 and again in the early sixties. You can see the Roman remains of Olicana in both the Manor House Museum next to the parish church, and in the Skipton Museum.

Above: THE PARISH CHURCH AND SAXON CROSSES
c1955 16001

The parish church of All Saints hides its history well. At first glance, the architecture is 19th century and confirms the rebuilding during 1860. However, the saxon crosses suggest a much earlier history. The porch to the church dates back to Norman times (13th century), the aisle from the 14th and the tower from the 15th century. A church is believed to have existed on this site in Saxon times circa AD700-800. Certainly the site was once the location of the Roman fort of Olicana, started in AD80 and rebuilt in stone during the 4th century.

Right: DETAIL FROM 16001

ALL SAINTS' CHURCH, THE NORMAN PORCH 1911 63568

This ornate Norman porch was expertly incorporated as a detail into the main body of the rebuilt church. To extend the nave during this rebuilding, the porch was moved, stone by stone, some ten feet towards the main road.

The town's Saxon crosses were originally scattered around the graveyard until they were brought together to make this unique feature. The central pillar dates from AD850, while the cross added in 1884 had been made from two separate stones, the lower part kept at

Myddleton Lodge and the upper part having been found in the river. Carvings on this pillar depict the four evangelists, St Matthew, Mark, Luke and John. All three are thought to have been burial monuments to important inhabitants, but the outer two had the ignominy of being used as gate posts, where they suffered much damage. All three were removed from the graveyard in 1983 and are now preserved safely away from the weather and pollution inside the tower where they remain on public display. At the same time, all the gravestones were taken to the cemetery and the area around the church grassed.

Wheatley village to the east is now merged with the main town, but in 1844, half a century before photograph 56490 was taken, four entrepreneurs from Leeds had not long before laid the foundations for the spa town. Ben Rhydding Hydro provided the impetus for a building boom that totally transformed this Wharfe village with unprecedented prosperity. Henceforth, the name Ben Rhydding subsumed the name of Wheatley. This fine church, (see 56490), was built at a cost of £10,000 on old cricket grounds at the turn of the century. St John's Church was then consecrated on 16th December 1905.

View 45160, pages 44-45, shows the oldest of Ilkley's four bridges across the Wharfe. This packhorse bridge was originally constructed in the early 17th century but following a massive flood had to be rebuilt in 1638. Yet again the fast flowing Wharfe swept it away; the present bridge - shown here - dates from 1675. While the Romans sufficed with a ford, the packhorse owners found much to complain about with the steep rise in the middle.

To facilitate the development of Middleton, it became clear that a new bridge across the Wharfe was necessary.

ST MARGARET'S CHURCH
1900 45156

This fine church in Queen's Road was consecrated on 10 September 1879 and was named after Margaret Snowdon, the daughter of the vicar of All Saints' Church. It was the second Anglican church in the town and is situated high on the moor side of town. Located bottom left, out of picture, are the three Panorama boulder stones thought to be some 3,500 years old and brought down from the moors in 1892. These Bronze Age relics are another example of Ilkley's past so very easily overlooked.

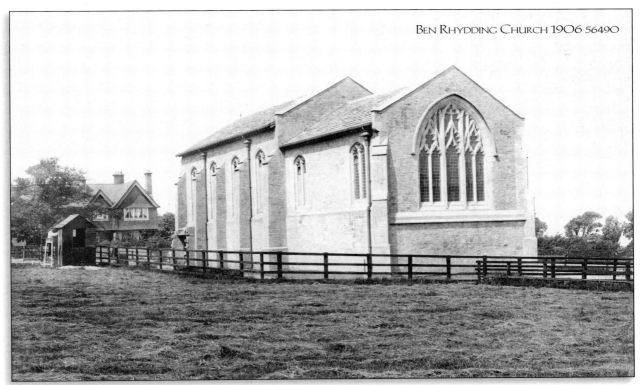

BEN RHYDDING CHURCH 1906 56490

EARLY MAN AND THE ROMANS

Constructed at a cost of £17,000, this was opened in June 1906 (see 56476, pages 48-49). First to cross was a contingent of soldiers from the 3rd Lancashire Royal Volunteers. Ilkley's other two bridges are further downstream. The suspension bridge opened in 1934, giving pedestrian access to Denton road and the bluebell woods of Middleton. Just past the stepping stones is the old Wheatley toll bridge between Ben Rhydding and Askwith, built in 1882. Mr Arthur Hill owned the bridge and took the tolls. After his death the Ilkley council purchased the structure and made it toll-free.

The cameraman uses a very wide-angle lens to create this deceptive picture - see 79055, pages 46-47.

The young girls are sitting in the gardens below the parish church, near the north gate to the old Roman Fort. The New Bridge is within the girls' view but is hidden here by the bush on the left. New Brook Street runs below the curve of the path and has yet to be developed to today's extent. The house on the right denotes the start of Weston Road and further down is the old Liberal Club, now the Playhouse Theatre. In line with the path is All Saints' Primary School in the original building of the old Ilkley National School's Infant School. The large houses on the banks of the river are the beginning of Ash Grove and Bath Street.

In between the toll and suspension bridges were some well-worn stepping stones (see 67327, page 52), giving cottage dwellers on the Askwith side access to Ilkley. In more recent years these gave walkers a delightful circular tour of the area. A number of the more worn stones have been replaced in the last few years, yet despite this, the width of the river at this point means a certain amount of courage is required to attempt this crossing.

The young lady by the fountain of the town's swimming pool (see 16004, page 53) suggests something we all remember - open-air baths tend to be chilly! Work

started on these new baths in July 1934 and although virtually completed by November, the opening was held over until the weather was more conducive to swimming. Invited guests were allowed a preview inspection on Friday 3rd May 1935 from 1pm to dusk and then at 3pm the following day came the official opening. Officiating was the Chairman of the Council, Dr M R Dobson, who thanked the builders and the architect, Ilkley's Surveyor, Mr A Skinner. A crowd of 3,000 was entertained by an exhibition of swimming and diving, with gramophone relayed on

THE BRIDGE 1900 45160

Behind the tree on the left of the photograph can be seen the old Middleton Hotel, completed in 1867. It became an officer's training school during the Second World War and then from 1947 was again in use as the Ilkley Moor Hotel. A fire in July 1968 destroyed the main building, but the building on the far left survived and remains popular as the Ilkley Moor Vaults - or the 'Taps'. Along the opposite bank, next to the present day garden centre, is the start of the 73 mile-long Dales Way to Bowness in the Lake District.

loudspeakers; Tom Barry, the Yorkshire Champion 1931-1933, showed off his diving prowess and then the Misses Mary, Joan and Nora Rigby displayed their graceful swimming. Miss Lily Cullingford then dived in to demonstrate more expert swim strokes, and this was followed by a mannequin parade by the 'Tudor' girls, who wore Tudor-style swimsuits. Then it was time for the children of Ilkley to enjoy their new pool and a mad rush followed for the free opening session.

Bank Holiday Monday was also free admission and even though charges were made for Sunday, the pool was still packed. The season's daily opening times were 7am to 9pm and 10pm on Wednesday and Sunday. The pool size is 75 feet by 30 feet, and in the main pool the depth ranges from six and a half to eight feet. The 325,000 gallons of water were heated to a uniform temperature of 65 degrees. Charges in the first year were Adults 6d and Children 4d. The pool was built at a total cost of £8669 and today is West Yorkshire's only remaining outdoor lido.

An indoor pool was later built adjacent to the lido to offer all year round swimming for the less hardy.

RIVER GARDENS 1925 79055

THE NEW BRIDGE 1906 56476

The Tea Gardens from Riverside Cafe c1965 16501

*Downstream from the old bridge, the Wharfe takes on
a gentle benign feel. Here pleasure boats can be hired in
the summer months. The landing stage has been in use
for over a hundred years and, together with the cafe and
children's amusements, draws visitors year after year to this
pastoral part of town. The Riverside Gardens retained their
popularity with day visitors as increasing affluence enabled
more families to use personal transport for recreation. In
the later view (16501), smart cars line up at the same time
as the Beeching axe is being sharpened. On many smaller
railway lines, the decline in custom throughout the 1950s
and 60s made eventual closure inevitable.*

The Riverside Cafe and Tea Gardens c1960 16052

The Riverside c1960 16051

The Riverside Cafe and Tea Gardens c1960 16055

The Stepping Stones 1914 67327

The Swimming Pool c1955 16004

Detail from 16004

THE WATER CURE

ILKLEY is sometimes referred to as the Malvern of the north; it was in Malvern in Gloucestershire that the concept of water therapy began in this country. Hydrotherapy emanated in Grafenburg, Austria in 1842, when a farmer first realised the power of cold water to relieve pain and disease. A tribute to this forward-thinking farmer, Vincent Priessnitz, can be found carved on a stone bath in the Canker Well garden at the west end of the Grove, just past the main shops. Northern businessmen from Leeds soon saw the potential of this new therapy and chose Ilkley as a centre for this new craze. The leader of the group, Hamer Stansfeld, a JP from Headingley, first engaged an Austrian practitioner to start hydrotherapy sessions in a boarding house in West View in March 1843. This was only a short distance from the White Wells and proved to be an instant success.

By 1844 Stansfeld's magnificent Ben Rhydding Hydro in nearby Wheatley village was opened for business. Here visitors were encouraged not only to drink two or three pints a day, but were also persuaded to bathe in it - all at near-freezing temperatures. Surprisingly Ilkley water contains nothing special in terms of nutrients but it was cold, pure and soft, and this was sufficient to convince guests of its power to heal. The water could also be drunk

WELLS HOUSE HOTEL
1900 45146

The £30,000 Wells House Hydro opened in May 1856. Designed by Cuthbert Brodrick, the architect of the Grand Hotel, Scarborough and the Leeds Town Hall, this splendid structure joined Ben Rhydding Hydro in putting Ilkley firmly on the water cure map. Guests were encouraged to walk up to the nearby White Wells and the Tarn, and because of this proximity to the Ilkley Moor, Wells House quickly established itself as a popular recuperation centre. Fresh air, exercise, good food and the majestic interior must have given even the feeblest guest an uplifting experience.

in quantity without ruining the appetite and, as an added attraction, it was a powerful diuretic.

The health regime called for a choice of either short daily plunges in a cold bath or long showers in the chilly water. These procedures were said to produce not only shivering and numbness but also a warm sense of light-headedness, sleepiness and a seizure of the joints! Once out of the water, the head would clear, leaving the bather feeling refreshed and invigorated; they might also glow with a new sense of high spirits and cheerfulness. The best time for a five-minute immersion was apparently in the morning before breakfast.

Another method of water therapy was to wrap the patient in wet sheets until they started to perspire profusely. At this point, they was stripped of the sheets and

quickly plunged into the cold bath. Rather surprisingly, visitors came back year after year for this harsh regime. Ben Rhydding proved so popular that other hydros were quickly established - fondly remembered names include the Wells House, Craiglands, the Grove Spa, Stoney Lea and the Troutbeck - and this spurred the first phase of the building boom in Ilkley.

These regimes, combined with the resort town's fresh air and plentiful walks, were almost certain to give even the most jaded a positive lift. Yet as the popularity increased each year so did the number of critics and disbelievers, and this may have contributed to the equally rapid decline of hydrotherapy. Charlatans and quacks invaded the town and brought much hostility between them and the established doctors. Within a few decades, hydros were forced to look for alternative customers. The tough daily regime was dropped in favour of comfort and relaxation. The Ben Rhydding built a golf course in 1885 and even installed a bar. Others became hotels and guesthouses. The Spa on the Grove seemed to prosper right up to its closure by offering a cafe and restaurant. Many were converted to flats and apartments or nursing homes, while others were simply demolished.

With the decline of the hydros in the early 1900s, owners looked for alternative attractions. The emphasis became more congenial with less of a medicinal feel, and during the 1930s, Victor Sylvester and his Orchestra entertained visitors staying in the town. Wells House ran as a hotel from the turn of the century until after the Second World War when it was purchased first by the Society of Jesuits; later, the Ministry of Labour used it as a hostel for volunteer workers. From 1952 it was a Domestic Science College and eventually became the Bradford and Ilkley Community College (see I6031, page 56). Since the College's departure a few years ago, the old Wells House Hydro has been redeveloped into luxury apartments.

THE WATER CURE

THE COLLEGE OF HOUSECRAFT c1955 16031

WELLS HOUSE HYDRO AND MOOR 1921 71282

Just a short walk from the Hydro and you are on Ilkley moor. In the top left of this photograph is the old Semon Convalescent Home.

56

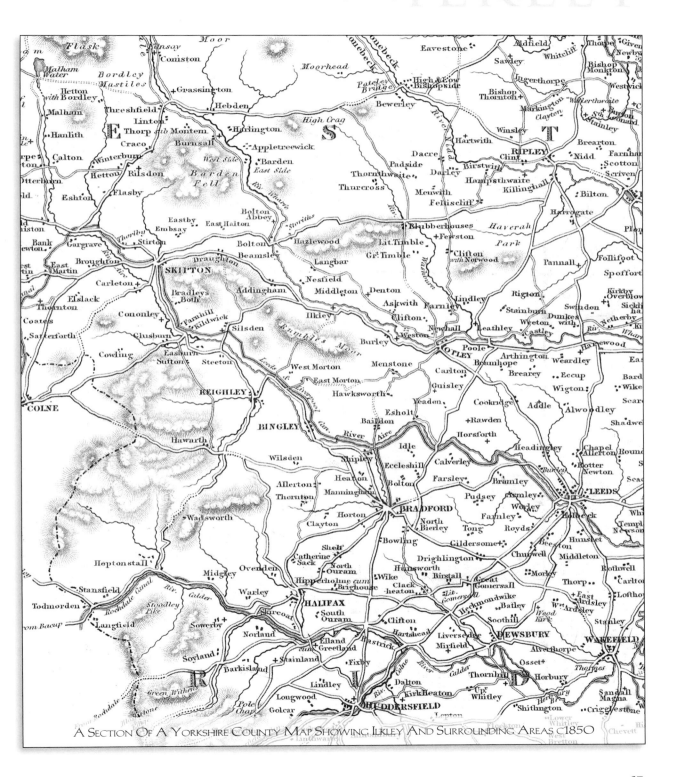

A Section Of A Yorkshire County Map Showing Ilkley And Surrounding Areas c1850

DAILY LIFE IN THE HYDRO

CRAIGLANDS 1900 45149

The imposing Craiglands Hydro on Cowpasture Road was opened in 1859, just three years after the Wells House Hydro. The surrounding gardens contained tennis and croquet facilities, together with delightful wooded walks. Originally forty guests were catered for, but this was extended to two hundred by the turn of the century. The huge ballroom was the venue for many lively balls. Craiglands remains the only hydro in the town to survive as a hotel.

Left: THE SEMON CONVALESCENT HOME c1874 7301

Opposite: MARLBOROUGH HOUSE 1900 45153
One of Ilkley's many smaller hydros, the Marlborough House on Clifton Road opened in 1878. It survived almost a century before being replaced by modern town houses in Marlborough Square.

DAILY LIFE IN THE HYDRO

ALTHOUGH the water from the springs around Ilkley is clear and sparkling, it also has no taste or smell. By the mid 1700s, the White Wells, 400ft above the main town, were attracting visitors because of remarkable claims being made for health cures, achieved either by drinking or bathing in the water.

A charity bath for people of reduced means was built near to White Wells and remains there today, albeit in a rather poor state. To bathe in the main White Wells daily cost 3s a week, but visitors could drink as much as they wished for no charge! The 1,160 gallons in each bath were used twice before being run off and refilled. A sitting room was available afterwards for relaxation. The Ilkley White Wells gave much relief to the ailing visitors and led to the eventual development of the first organised hydrotherapy establishments, which were far more palatial premises. Once these came into existence, the old White Wells, although still in use, took on a much-reduced role in the town.

Life in the big new hydros was fairly regimented. Inside Ben Rhydding, the daily routine consisted of a strict regime of healthy eating with no spices, pepper or mustard allowed. The eighty patients could expect to take breakfast at 8am, followed by the reading of the scriptures. The remainder of the morning was filled with bathing or perhaps a gentle stroll in the fresh valley air. Lunch was served at 2pm and then relaxation was encouraged for the afternoon. Guests feeling fairly robust could arrange for further baths to be provided. Evening dinner was taken at 7pm prompt and then at 10pm all the gas lights in the public rooms were turned off. Guests were expected to be in bed by 11pm. A stay in the beautiful surroundings with its wonderful gardens cost three guineas a week. Other less grand hydros offered a similar week's stay for two guineas.

DAILY LIFE IN THE HYDRO

A merchant from Bradford and former Mayor, Charles Semon, built Ilkley's Convalescent Home to serve working people of slender means (see 7301, page 58). He recognised that many of the hydros and homes catered mainly for the wealthy, but he felt that as the workers had helped create that wealth through their toil, they should also be offered recuperation and relaxation away from the poverty ridden streets of the West Riding mill towns. Shown here in the year of its opening, the Semon Home promised a healthy regime of good food, rest and kind treatment, together with medical attention, all for a weekly charge of ten shillings.

In 1876 Semon gave the house to the Bradford Corporation, who continued to use it until closure and demolition, despite much local opposition in 1995. Private housing now occupies this moor-side site.

Built in 1880 at the corner of Cowpasture Road and Ben Rhydding Road, the Stoney Lea Hydro (67325, below) also offered guests the usual relaxing diversions, like croquet and tennis. A former bath man from the nearby Ben Rhydding Hydro was the owner until its sale in 1945, whereupon it became a hotel. After many subsequent changes in ownership, with each proprietor trying to devise a successful format for the enterprise, the hotel finally closed in 1981, when it was demolished and replaced by town houses.

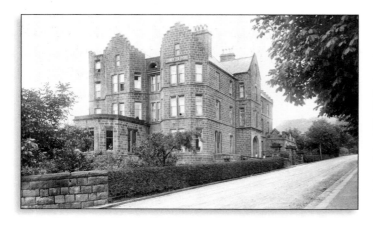

STONEY LEA HYDRO 1914 67325

THE ROYAL HOTEL 1914 67324

Within easy distance of the railway station, the Royal Hotel served Ilkley's many visitors for nearly a century. It was built on the site of Mother Downes' charming thatched cottage in 1872 and was much enlarged twenty years later. At the time of closure, the thought of conversion to apartments was not yet fashionable. Demolition came in 1962 and the site was used for Wells Court and Wells Mews.

ENTERTAINING THE VISITORS

VISITORS to Ilkley had no trouble finding daily entertainment. Henry Wray's Pleasure Gardens down by the river offered dancing in the Pavilion, with a fine collection of birds and animals in the Aviary and Monkey House. The Arcadia Bandstand in Wells Road presented Pierrot shows daily through the season at 3pm and 8pm - 'come rain or shine'. Here there was dancing on the boarded floor and, with a constant change of programme, visitors flocked in, paying charges ranging from 9d right down to 2d. The King's Hall mixed variety and musical evenings with animated pictures, with 'Smoking Permitted' - a key selling point!

Ilkley's first purpose-built full-time cinema opened in Back Grove on Friday 21 February 1913. The Picture House was advertised as Cosy Corner and only screened films of the 'Highest Grade'. The Grove Picture House held 400 (later increased to 800) on a sloping floor and was fully fireproofed throughout. A pianist and violinist provided musical accompaniment to the silent films. Seats in the gallery and at the back of the stalls were tip-up and upholstered in velvet. On the opening night, most of the seats were occupied and the privilege of being allowed to smoke was one that those men present greatly appreciated! The opening films consisted of travel films around Canada, taking in sights such as the Niagara Falls. Other shorts included 'The Fire Fighter's Love', 'A Girl of the West', 'Clothes Make the Man', 'Bunny's Suicide', 'The Window Cleaner', 'His Too Faithful Friend' and 'Jim Mistaken for Foolshead'. Miss Lofthouse from Burley was the nimble pianist keeping up with all the mood changes. Matinees for children began on the Saturday afternoon with prices of 1d, 2d,and 3d. The Grove and the King's Hall battled it out to offer patrons the finest films but the King's Hall suffered for not being just a cinema. Other venues licensed for cinema shows during 1914 were the St Margaret's Church Hall and the Bridge Street Pavilion.

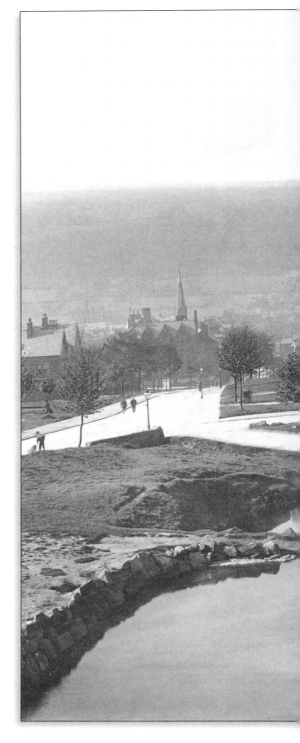

WEST VIEW 1900 45158

At the top of Wells Road, as the town turns to moor land, lies this delightful area, ideal for a little perambulation. Children could paddle in the pond and then skip over the heather to the nearby Tarn.

An altogether more grand entertainment centre later opened in Railway Road. The New Cinema, Café and Ballroom were built on part of the old cricket ground and opened to the gleeful public on Monday 21st May 1928. Starring in the opening film, '7th Heaven' were Janet Gayner and Charles Farrel. In 1948, the Grove started the Ilkley Young Citizen's Matinee Club. Over 500 children were in the opening audience, when they were encouraged to adhere to certain rules, such as speaking the truth, being thoughtful and kind.

In spite of this popularity, by the mid-1960s most cinemas were struggling against the competition from television. Both Ilkley's cinemas closed within twenty months of each other. The writing was on the wall for the Grove when, after the death of the proprietor, planning permission was refused to convert the building to retail shops. However, the council did express an interest in acquiring the property as part of the town's central development. So within a few months the Grove finally closed its doors, marking its end with a 3-day showing of the biblical epic 'The Greatest Story Ever Told', starring Max Von Sydow and Charlton Heston. The final show commenced at 6.30pm on Saturday 30 December 1967. The last manager, Mr J E Akroyd, was then transferred to the Beech Hill Cinema in Otley. The Grove was demolished within a few weeks of closure and the site is now part of the central car park.

The New Cinema, renamed the Essoldo in the 1950s, lasted until 1969, when it closed on Saturday 6 September, half-full with six hundred people enjoying Michael Caine in 'The Italian Job'. Demolition started on Monday 15th September and a new supermarket was then built on the site, which is now occupied by Sunwin House. Ilkley's original cinema, the King's Hall, remains in use today as a well-patronised, multi-purpose entertainment complex.

THE MOOR C1965 16095

One of the many streams that cascade off the moor - this is the beginning of Mill Ghyll, which flows down Wells Road and then underneath Brook Street. The old bridge still remains and the steps on the right lead to the Craig Tarn, formed from a former bog.

ENTERTAINING THE VISITORS

Right: HOLLYBROOK GUEST HOUSE c1955 16017

Situated on the corner of Queen's Road and Westwood Drive, this guest house was also a victim of changing times. For many years it was run as a Methodist guesthouse, and Alan Titchmarsh's mother worked here for a number of happy years. The Hollybrook closed in the late 1970s and was demolished in 1980. New houses now occupy the site, but the adjoining cottage still remains.

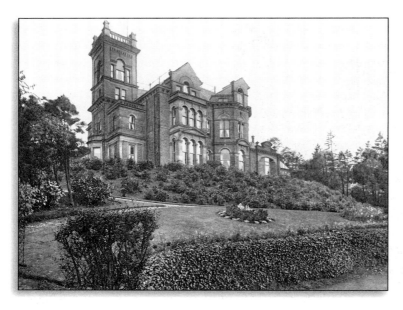

Above: ARDENLEA, THE RAILWAYMEN'S CONVALESCENT HOME 1925 77874

A fascinating history lies behind Ardenlea, high up on Queen's Drive. The house, which has splendid views over the town and valley towards Middleton, was built as a family home in 1881 for Mr and Mrs George Thorpe. Just before the First World War, it was taken over by the North Eastern Railway Company as a convalescent home for railway workers, not only from the NER but all the other great companies. The official opening was held on 8th May 1915 and it served the industry well until closure in 1963, when it was purchased by the Marie Curie Foundation. This organisation moved to new premises in 2001 and the building has been totally renovated to form nine private apartments. It has been renamed Thorpe Hall after its original owners.

ENTERTAINING THE VISITORS

WEST VIEW PARK 1906 56479

WEST VIEW PARK 1906 56479

In the middle of West View Park, opposite the paddling pool, was the bandstand. Here at the turn of the century visitors were entertained by Pierrot shows and bands. To the left is Wells House. The gardens, devoid of the bandstand since the 1960s, are now enjoying a new lease of life as the Darwin Gardens, named after Charles Darwin, a visitor to Wells House in 1859 at the time of his writing 'The Origin of Species'.

THE TARN 1900 45157A

ENTERTAINING THE VISITORS

WEST VIEW PARK 1914 67329

One can almost smell the fragrance of the heather that adds to the enjoyment of this pre-war concert. The gathering rain clouds are no worry to the band, as the wooden shelter provides plenty of cover.

THE TARN 1923 74476

Improving on nature, the Victorians created two tarns out of muddy bogs on this part of Ilkley moor shown in 45157A, pages 68-69, both within easy walking distance of the town. The one in this photograph is both lower and larger, and more accessible. Victorian children search for tiddlers, while their elders consider their constitution. During the winter months, the tarn occasionally freezes, and this must have delighted the Victorian ice-skaters. In 74476 we are above the Tarn looking out over the Wharfe Valley. Craiglands is on the right, while on the far left Wells House can be glimpsed.

ENTERTAINING THE VISITORS

THE MOORS 1914 67335

On the way up to the White Wells, a man and his dog pause to drink in the dramatic view. Meanwhile the ladies sense the Tearoom just around the corner. This small white building still stands, although in a rather dilapidated state. Added to the White Wells in 1829, it was used as the Charity Bath.

ENTERTAINING THE VISITORS

The prospect revealed in view 67334 (right) offers refreshment for the soul, with a stunning outlook all the way up the valley and over to Whernside. In 1914 visitors would still walk up from the town to the so-called Roman Baths for an immersion in the chilly waters. Photograph 63563 (see page 76) shows one of the two Roman-style plunge baths inside the White House. There is no evidence that the Romans knew about the spring and its healing properties, but the name has a romantic and meaningful ring to it. Visitors could use these facilities on payment of 6d a douche. Each plunge bath contained 1,150 gallons and the temperature was a constant 40° F - not far above freezing! This bath can still be viewed at weekends but the second is now covered over.

WHITE WELLS AND MOORLAND INN 1921 *71275*

The Wells House Hydro on the right of these views gives an idea of how compact the town is. A stroll up to the wells remains a great attraction, although sadly Mrs Williamson's café was pulled down in the 1960s.

74

FROM THE WHITE WELLS 1914 67334

WHITE WELLS AND MOORS 1921 71274

WHITE WELLS, ROMAN BATH 1911 63563

ENTERTAINING THE VISITORS

Above: THE MOORS 1906 56482

This captivating view was taken looking towards the top of the 1,320-feet-high Rombalds Moor and shows White Wells at top right. The rustic bridge, now rather more plain, points the path towards Panorama rocks, from where visitors could complete their circular tour of southern Ilkley, down Heber's Ghyll, passing the Chalybeate springs on the way.

Left: WHITE WELLS C1955 16010

This photograph captures the very essence of Ilkley - the moors, the town nestling in the valley and the gentle slopes of Middleton in the distance.

SOME LOCAL LORE

THE HERMIT INN at Burley Woodhead is today the only reminder of a colourful local character: Job Senior. He was the hermit of Rombalds Moor - a dishevelled farm-worker who singularly failed to attract much female attention. Yet at the age of 60, he set his sights on and married 80-year old Mary Barrett, who owned a nearby smallholding complete with cottage, field and vegetable garden. Some years later Mary died and Job assumed he would inherit the estate, but her relatives had other ideas. They managed to disinherit him and he was left with only the cottage. Even worse, one day he returned to find the cottage had been destroyed and his meagre savings stolen. His determined streak encouraged him to use the stone to build a primitive shelter and it was here that he lived for many years. He became a local celebrity and visitors would come to hear him sing. Coins were tossed his way as reward. Sadly, the harsh life on the moors took its toll and he eventually became ill and was offered a barn behind the Wheatsheaf in Church Street. Within a few days he was transferred to the workhouse in Carlton near Otley, where he died in 1857 at the age of 77. His grave can be found in the Burley churchyard.

THE MOORS 1914 67333

Behind the Cow and Calf rocks is this desolate valley from where most of the stone to build the town was quarried. Hangingstone Quarry was the site of a huge enterprise that saw the destruction of the giant Bull Rock. The massive rocks were taken down Cowpasture Road to stone breaking yards around Ash Grove.

DENTON PARK FROM COW AND CALF ROCKS 1914 67330

This young man looks out from between these famous rocks towards the magnificent estate of Denton Park.

SOME LOCAL LORE

The seat of the Fairfax family, the present-day Denton Hall, is the third such home on the site. The first, built in the 14th century, was destroyed by fire, as was the second in 1734. Owned in the 13th century by the Vavasours, by the 15th century it belonged to the Thwaite family. The marriage in 1515 at Bolton Percy of Sir William of Steeton to Isabel Thwaite, a nun at Appleton Monastery, subsequently brought the estate under the Fairfax family. This fortuitous marriage also brought with it land at Keighley, Askwith, the centre of York, and later Nun Appleton and Bolton Percy. The present house was constructed in 1735 to the designs of the respected York architect John Carr using stone from a local quarry. The first Lord Fairfax, Thomas, is buried in a tomb inside Otley Church. Denton Hall was used as the location for the film, 'The Water Babies'.

'On ilkla moor baht 'at...' So where did that song come from? Well the tune is from the hymn, Cranbrook. It's reputed that in 1886 a church choir from Halifax was holding its summer picnic high up on the moors. One of their young girls, called Mary Jane, wandered off with her sweetheart. When they returned, they were rather embarrassed as the choir burst into song with the first line 'Where's tha bin since Ah saw thee? Tha's been a courting Mary Jane'. Many artists have subsequently performed the song, perhaps none more unusual than a Russian choir at the Drury Lane Theatre in London, who sang it in their own language with the opening line 'Znai Je My Videli Tebia'.

Through the rocks in 74475, pages 80-81, we see the original village of Wheatley, subsumed for over a century by the Ben Rhydding Hydro, which can be seen centre right. Once the water cure boom had passed, the hydro became a golf hotel from 1885. It continued in this resort-style throughout the early part of the last century up to the Second World War. After this, the War Department requisitioned it. From 1945 it remained empty until, sadly,

VIEW FROM THE COW AND CALF ROCKS 1923 74475

demolition became inevitable. The end came in 1955 in a decade that saw many other fine old West Riding houses lost due to high maintenance costs and death duties. Here in Ben Rhydding, houses were built on part of the site. The golf course remains, as does the name Hydro Close. A marble bath, part of a fountain in the grounds, was taken to the Canker Well at the end of the Grove and can still be seen today.

Past the Cow and Calf rocks, you'll find at High Eldwick Dick Hudson's public house (see 71288, pages 84-85). By road it is seven miles from Ilkley, but over

the top you could walk to it in four. To the thousands of mill workers who came here on hot summer days, it was famous for its Yorkshire puddings that cost 1 shilling each, the Ploughman's lunch for 2d or the tasty ham and eggs tea served until 11pm. The hostelry is built on the old packhorse route from Bingley to Ilkley. Originally on this site was a farm, run by Thomas Hudson and his family from 1809 to 1895. Nearby was the Plough Inn, but with the building of a new and better road, the licence was transferred from here to Hudson's Highgate Farm, which was renamed the Fleece Inn

- which remains its official name to this day. Thomas's son Dick took over the inn from 1850 and built up the recreation trade for the workers from nearby Aire valley. Dick died in 1878. An Austrian proprietor then wanted to turn the grounds into a pleasure garden complete with fountain, but was unsuccessful. In 1900, the old pub was demolished and the new one built. Because of its isolated location, one of the landlords was keen on illegal brewing, yet his efforts came to an end after being fined at Bingley magistrates. Today, Dick Hudson's remains a popular venue for ramblers.

SOME LOCAL LORE

THE MOORS 1914 67339

Up above the Cow and Calf rocks is more evidence of quarrying, but in this photograph the heather softens the scene for the Edwardian picnickers taking in the valley view, top right.

VIEW OF SWASTIKA STONE 1914 67341

In this photograph you can see the top of the Semon Convalescent Home just beyond the reservoir. A fair walk westwards then brings you to the Swastika Stone, which is unique in this country. Other examples have been found in Tossene in Sweden and Mycenae in Greece and all depict fertility and religious symbols. The council placed the iron railing around the site in 1913.

Above: COW AND CALF ROCKS
1921 71283

It is well worth the effort to climb up these rocks: you're on top of the world, if a little weary and overheated. Luckily, just below refreshments are to hand at the Cow and Calf Inn, formerly known as the Highfield.

Left: DETAIL FROM 71283

NAMES OF SUBSCRIBERS

The following people have kindly supported this book by purchasing limited edition copies prior to publication.

Richard and Sietske Archer

Pete, Steph, Tom, Will, Em and Fi Atkinson

Lord A Nonni-Maus Bart A T

The Bartlett Family, Malm House, Ilkley

Mrs Muriel Bell

Mrs E Bott, Ilkley

Mr & Mrs R P Bott, Guiseley, Yorks

Mr & Mrs A J Bott, Farnham, Hants

Mr & Mrs T M Bott, Farnworth, Lancs

Jane Bowden from Mother

Mr and Mrs W Bowness, Ilkley

Mr & Mrs M C Brook, Kalamunda, Australia

F Brown & family, formerly Burley in Wharfedale

In memory of a dear son, Richard 13/12/51 - 19/11/04

In memory of a dear husband and father, Richard
13/12/51 - 19/11/04

In memory of a dear brother and uncle, Richard
13/12/51 - 19/11/04

John and Monika Butler

Iain and Suzanne Candlish of Highwood

Rose Evelyn Clark, born Ilkley 9/10/1937

Raymond Clark, born 7th April 1971, Ilkley

Jean Clark, born 25/04/1957, Ilkley

Nigel & Jennifer Cottam

John and Barbara Cox, Hexham

The Crawshaw-Gammon Family, Ilkley

Deborah, on your 44th birthday, from Mum

Mr & Mrs P W Dickinson, Ilkley

Mr & Mrs B H Dickinson, Kingswinford

The John G Dobson Family, Ilkley

Winton Evans from Mother

The Fearnley Family, Stead Hall Farm, Woodhead

Maggie and Dave Gilbert, Ilkley

The Gilroy Family, Ilkley

Sally Gunton, Burley in Wharfedale

To Jonathan, Hayley, Harry and Eleanor

Kathleen Hinchcliffe

Michael Hirst

Kathleen Horner from Auntie Mabel

The Hume Family

In memory of Eric and Margaret Hunnebell

Reginald Frederick Jones

Robert Kehoe

Garry Lambert and family of Ilkley

Nigel, Judy, Chris, Andrew and Betty Law

To Anthony Laycock on his Birthday

To my husband Graham, love Victoria Lowes

To Margaret and Childhood Memories

Paul, Julie, Emily and Oliver Moulton 2006

To Mum & Dad, love Julie, Paul, Em & Oli, 06

Peter and Kathleen Murray, Ilkley

Betty Patchett

Antony Edward Peacock, February 2006

William Garrard Pitt, Ilkley

Matthew Pitt, Thorp Arch - Born Ilkley 1964

Richard, Happy Birthday, love Julie

Mr & Mrs J J Richards of Ilkley

Mr & Mrs K Roberts, Bedford, USA

To Ron on your 70th Birthday, love A & C

The Saxton Family, Ilkley

Mr & Mrs P J Scott

Tony and Sylvia Scull

Joyce & Jack Spurr, Ben Rhydding, Ilkley

To Jim Taylor, love from all of us xxx

To Mick Ware, Ilkley, on his 60th Birthday

Jackie Lu Wilkinson

D G & J Wilson

R M & C A Wood, Christine Robert Wood

William Wilkinson Wright. A man who liked hard work.

INDEX

FRITH PRODUCTS & SERVICES

Francis Frith would doubtless be pleased to know that the pioneering publishing venture he started in 1860 still continues today. Over a hundred and forty years later, The Francis Frith Collection continues in the same innovative tradition and is now one of the foremost publishers of vintage photographs in the world. Some of the current activities include:

Interior Decoration

Today Frith's photographs can be seen framed and as giant wall murals in thousands of pubs, restaurants, hotels, banks, retail stores and other public buildings throughout the country. In every case they enhance the unique local atmosphere of the places they depict and provide reminders of gentler days in an increasingly busy and frenetic world.

Product Promotions

Frith products are used by many major companies to promote the sales of their own products or to reinforce their own history and heritage. Frith promotions have been used by Hovis bread, Courage beers, Scots Porage Oats, Colman's mustard, Cadbury's foods, Mellow Birds coffee, Dunhill pipe tobacco, Guinness, and Bulmer's Cider.

Genealogy and Family History

As the interest in family history and roots grows world-wide, more and more people are turning to Frith's photographs of Great Britain for images of the towns, villages and streets where their ancestors lived; and, of course, photographs of the churches and chapels where their ancestors were christened, married and buried are an essential part of every genealogy tree and family album.

Frith Products

All Frith photographs are available Framed or just as Mounted Prints and Posters (size 23 x 16 inches). These may be ordered from the address below. From time to time other products - Address Books, Calendars, Table Mats, etc - are available.

The Internet

Already ninety thousand Frith photographs can be viewed and purchased on the internet through the Frith websites and a myriad of partner sites.

For more detailed information on Frith companies and products, look at these sites:

www.francisfrith.co.uk
www.francisfrith.com
(for North American visitors)

See the complete list of Frith Books at:

www.francisfrith.co.uk

This web site is regularly updated with the latest list of publications from The Francis Frith Collection. If you wish to buy books relating to another part of the country that your local bookshop does not stock, you may purchase on-line.

For further information, trade, or author enquiries please contact us at the address below:
The Francis Frith Collection, Frith's Barn, Teffont, Salisbury, Wiltshire, England SP3 5QP.
Tel: +44 (0)1722 716 376 Fax: +44 (0)1722 716 881 Email: sales@francisfrith.co.uk

See Frith books on the internet at www.francisfrith.co.uk

FREE PRINT OF YOUR CHOICE

Mounted Print
Overall size 14 x 11 inches (355 x 280mm)

Choose any Frith photograph in this book.
Simply complete the Voucher opposite and return it with your remittance for £2.25 (to cover postage and handling) and we will print the photograph of your choice in SEPIA (size 11 x 8 inches) and supply it in a cream mount with a burgundy rule line (overall size 14 x 11 inches).
Please note: photographs with a reference number starting with a "Z" are not Frith photographs and cannot be supplied under this offer.
Offer valid for delivery to one UK address only.

PLUS: **Order additional Mounted Prints at HALF PRICE - £7.49 each** (normally £14.99)
If you would like to order more Frith prints from this book, possibly as gifts for friends and family, you can buy them at half price (with no additional postage and handling costs).

PLUS: **Have your Mounted Prints framed**
For an extra £14.95 per print you can have your mounted print(s) framed in an elegant pol-ished wood and gilt moulding, overall size 16 x 13 inches (no additional postage and handling required).

IMPORTANT!

These special prices are only available if you use this form to order. You must use the ORIGINAL VOUCHER on this page (no copies permitted). We can only despatch to one UK address. This offer cannot be combined with any other offer.

Send completed Voucher form to:
The Francis Frith Collection, Frith's Barn, Teffont, Salisbury, Wiltshire SP3 5QP

CHOOSE A PHOTOGRAPH FROM THIS BOOK

Voucher for **FREE** and Reduced Price Frith Prints

Please do not photocopy this voucher. Only the original is valid, so please fill it in, cut it out and return it to us with your order.

Picture ref no	Page no	Qty	Mounted @ £7.49	Framed + £14.95	Total Cost £
		1	Free of charge*	£	£
			£7.49	£	£
			£7.49	£	£
			£7.49	£	£
			£7.49	£	£
			£7.49	£	£

Please allow 28 days for delivery. Offer available to one UK address only

* Post & handling	£2.25
Total Order Cost	£

Title of this book . . . .

I enclose a cheque/postal order for £ . . . .
made payable to 'The Francis Frith Collection'

OR please debit my Mastercard / Visa / Maestro card, details below

Card Number

Issue No (Maestro only)   Valid from (Maestro)

Expires   Signature

Name Mr/Mrs/Ms . . . .

Address . . . .

. . . .

. . . .

. . . . Postcode . . . .

Daytime Tel No . . . .

Email . . . .

ISBN 1-84589-127-9   Valid to 31/12/08

Free Print – see overleaf

Can you help us with information about any of the Frith photographs in this book?

We are gradually compiling an historical record for each of the photographs in the Frith archive. It is always fascinating to find out the names of the people shown in the pictures, as well as insights into the shops, buildings and other features depicted.

If you recognize anyone in the photographs in this book, or if you have information not already included in the author's caption, do let us know. We would love to hear from you, and will try to publish it in future books or articles.

Our production team

Frith books are produced by a small dedicated team at offices in the converted Grade II listed 18th-century barn at Teffont near Salisbury, illustrated above. Most have worked with The Francis Frith Collection for many years. All have in common one quality: they have a passion for The Francis Frith Collection. The team is constantly expanding, but currently includes:

Andrew Alsop, Paul Baron, Jason Buck, John Buck, Jenny Coles, Heather Crisp, David Davies, Natalie Davis, Louis du Mont, Isobel Hall, Chris Hardwick, Julian Hight, Peter Horne, James Kinnear, Karen Kinnear, Tina Leary, Stuart Login, Sue Molloy, Sarah Roberts, Kate Rotondetto, Eliza Sackett, Terence Sackett, Sandra Sampson, Adrian Sanders, Sandra Sanger, Julia Skinner, Lewis Taylor, Will Tunnicliffe, David Turner and Ricky Williams.